Customer at the Crossroads

From Parable to Practice

Barbara "BJ" Hateley & Eric Harvey

Illustrated by John Grimes

Dedicated To
WARREN H. SCHMIDT,
author, poet, filmmaker, consultant, professor,
mentor, friend ... and inspiration!

CUSTOMER at the CROSSROADS
From Parable to Practice

Distributed by

The WALK THE TALK® Company

ORDERING INFORMATION

Order copies of CUSTOMER at the CROSSROADS from The WALK THE TALK Company
by ...

Phone: **1.888.822.9255**, Monday - Friday, 8:30 AM - 5:00 PM, Central
or Internet: **www.walkthetalk.com**

Or, reproduce and complete the order form in the back, and send it by ...

Fax: 972.243.0815
or Mail: The WALK THE TALK Company
2925 LBJ Freeway, Suite 201
Dallas, TX 75234

Printed in the United States of America
10 9 8 7 6 5 4 3 2

Printed by The Graphics Group

 This book is printed on recycled paper.

FOREWORD

If there is anything we in business talk about these days, it's customer service. Books, videos, seminars and consultants abound – and yet we all know that the way we personally are treated is getting worse. And inside our organizations? If we are in leadership, we bemoan the lack of good people. If we are on the front line, we complain about the lack of leadership.

Personally, I'm convinced that today's organizations are filled at all levels with good people, who truly do want to be of service. It would be self-defeating to deliberately set out to give bad service! Why then are you and I not experiencing improved service – excellent service – from all types of organizations?

As with all truths, the answer is obvious to understand, but not always easy to act on. What *is* easy is to say the right things: "The customer is the reason for our business!" "The customer is always right!" "We value your business!" "Satisfaction guaranteed!" But as we only too ruefully know, doing the right things is quite another matter. The handful of organizations which have mastered doing the right things they are saying, day in and day out, from one customer to the next, have been elevated to sainthood by the customers. Sainthood and, not incidentally, sustained business success. Disney, Federal Express, Southwest and Nordstrom all come to mind. They enjoy a rich partnership with their customers, while the rest of us fall into the also-ran category, our expensive service initiatives all for naught.

In one of his most oft-quoted statements, Warren Bennis reminds us: "Managers do things right. Leaders do the right things." This is especially true of customer service delivery. Service leaders do the right things! If you desire to be seen as a service leader at whatever level of the organization, you must do the right things. Identifying and doing those right things is what this book is about.

BJ Hateley and Eric Harvey have made a gift to us of this small book and simple book. But don't be deceived. These few words are all pearls – and they are invitations to action. The right action. If you heed the wisdom of this story, you will learn profound lessons to apply in your organization. You will become the only true kind of change agent there is – the person who knows that we must *be* the change we want to see in the world.

An ancient Chinese proverb reminds us that "the longest journey begins with the first step." On the journey to customer service excellence, reading this book and living what you learn is a firm first step.

Heartfelt best wishes and heart-warming blessings to you on this journey. See you on the road!

Betsy Sanders
Former Vice-President and General Manager, Nordstrom
Author of Fabled Service

Our story begins in the land of Business as Usual, a place familiar to one and all. It was here that Customer lived— *A. Customer*, to be more precise.

 His needs were simple, his wants were few; just the basics would make him happy. He wanted to buy things; shirts and shoes, food and fun, supplies and staples— the usual stuff.

But the sales people sometimes seemed too busy when A. Customer came along. They were often so involved in their own conversations, they didn't even notice him!

Once in a while, A. Customer had a problem: something needed fixing; something needed exchanging; a rug needed cleaning; a chair needed upholstering. Nothing extraordinary, just simple stuff.

But the customer service people, who were supposedly there to help, weren't always so helpful. They would pass A. Customer all around the Land of Business as Usual, sending him from person... to person... to person.

Or, they would tell him to fill out lo-o-o-ng forms and answer questions before they would pay attention to him. Everyone seemed to think A. Customer was just a lot of trouble.

"This would be a great place to work," they all said, "if only it weren't for A. Customer."

Life in the Land of Business as Usual was difficult for A. Customer. Disappointment and frustration seemed to be his fate.

Was there nothing he could do, he often wondered. Did no one care about his wants and needs?

Finally one day, he decided to try a new place... it was on the outskirts of Business as Usual. "Maybe things will be different here," he thought as he walked through their door. "After all, this place is new."

$\mathbb{B}$ut alas, his hopes were soon dashed...

The place was new, the product was new, the people were new – but the story was old.

It was the same old story of Business as Usual.

He turned on his heel and bolted out the door.

"I've had it with
Business As Usual!" he shouted.
"I'm leaving! There must be a better place *somewhere!*"

And he headed down the road just as fast as his legs would carry him. He walked and he walked and he walked, putting more and more distance between himself and the Land of Business as Usual.

After a while, he came to a fork in the road.

"Well, now," he puzzled, "which way should I go?"

He read the signpost and considered his options.

"The Land of Catchy Slogans, the Land of Big Promises, the Land of Lofty Vision... Hmmm, which way to go?"

"Well, let's see," he mused, "The Land of Catchy Slogans — that one sounds interesting. I'll bet they have great musical jingles and nifty banners and buttons. It will be a wonderful place. I think I could be happy there."

So, down the road he went, eager to join the festivities.

"What fun," he thought as he got closer and caught sight of the balloons, colored lights, and brightly painted signs. The flags flapping in the breeze seemed to be welcoming him to come on in.

And indeed, everyone was having a great time, patting themselves on the back for their great teamwork, giving prizes, special awards, and Employee of the Month parking spaces.

There was celebration all around.

"Excuse me," he said, tapping someone on the shoulder. "Is there someone here I could talk to?"

"Sure, sure. Have a button," came the reply.

"No, I don't need a button. I came because..." A. Customer continued.

"Here, have a balloon!" came the response, before he could even finish.

"You're number one with us!" a chorus of voices chimed in his ears.

"You don't understand..." he tried to explain.

But it was no use. The music blared, the banners flew, and the balloons bobbed cheerfully in the air. But no one stopped to see what it was that A. Customer really wanted.

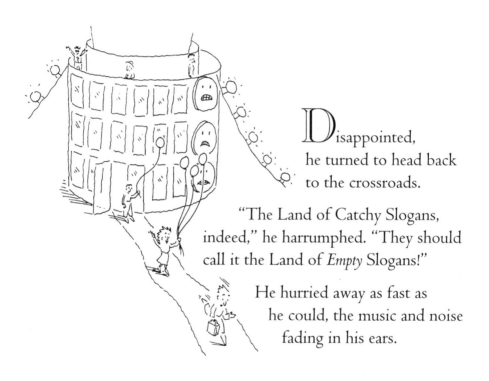

Disappointed,
he turned to head back
to the crossroads.

"The Land of Catchy Slogans,
indeed," he harrumphed. "They should
call it the Land of *Empty* Slogans!"

He hurried away as fast as
he could, the music and noise
fading in his ears.

"Where to now?" he thought as he arrived at the fork in the road and looked again at the signpost.

"I'm sure one of these places must be right for me.... Hmmm. The Land of Big Promises.... Could this be a place that really means it when they promise to stand behind their products and their services? That would sure be something new!"

"I'm going to go check it out," he said to himself as he hurried down the road.

Soon he arrived at a large, sparkling building of steel and glass. As he stepped through the double glass doors, he heard the beeping and chirping of office machines and he saw mile-high stacks of forms and papers all over the place. There were cardboard boxes, imprinted with a snazzy colorful logo, whizzing along conveyor belts stretching hither and yon.

"Welcome to the Land of Big Promises," beeped a computerized voice from a speaker phone. "Service, quality, and instant delivery — all yours with just a press of the button. Pick up the phone, press #1 followed by the $*$ sign, and place your order."

A. Customer was startled, for he saw no people. He heard only this disembodied voice from the phone, surrounded by computers, machines of all types, and those endlessly moving conveyor belts.

"Well, I came because of your promise to stand behind your products," he replied after pressing #1 and *.

"Ah, yes, indeed," the voice on the phone said. "Just press #3 now. We promise that our products are the very best, and our service is smooth and efficient. Now press #2, wait for the beep, press *77, and then take the printout from the printer to your left."

And with that, a legal-looking form rolled out of the printer.

"Now, sign on the bottom line, then press ###, and insert the printout in the slot to your right," the phone continued.

As he signed his name, and pushed the paper through the slot, a bell rang, a red light flashed... and the conveyor belt dropped a heavy package at A. Customer's feet.

"But this isn't exactly what I had in mind," he protested to the phone.

"Sorry," the phone replied. "No custom orders. You wanted quality and speed — we delivered. What you see is what you get. No exchanges; no returns. Policies are policies. I don't make the rules, I just follow them."

"But, but...," A. Customer stammered.

"Didn't you read the fine print?" the phone said matter-of-factly. "Please dial 9 to get out."

Stunned and disappointed, A. Customer hung up the phone as he muttered, "You don't stand behind your products, you *hide* behind them!"

Out through the double glass doors he went. "The Land of Big Promises, indeed," he sputtered. "They oughta call it the Land of *Broken* Promises."

And he headed back to the crossroads.

He gazed up at the sign again and realized he had only one option left — The Land of Lofty Vision.

"Well, it sounds encouraging," he thought. "A place with vision will see how important I am. They'll take good care of me."

So down the road he went once more, hoping against hope that this was the place he was looking for. "They're bound to do the right thing," he thought as he walked, his feelings of hope mixed with quiet desperation.

Land of Lofty Vision

As he drew closer, A. Customer could hear a deep resonant voice over the loudspeaker. A big crowd was gathered, listening to their President's inspiring words. Everyone was captivated by the magnificent vision he had for their land.

"Excuse me," A. Customer started to say.

"Sshhh," someone hissed at him. "We're working on our Vision here. Can't you see this is important?"

"But, but...I've come such a long way to get here," he replied.

"Sshhh! Sshhh!" Several of them turned and scowled. "Our Vision is our future!"

"Your *future?*" A. Customer asked incredulously. "But what about the *present?* I'm here right now!"

"Puh-leeze," they responded. "Not now!" And they "shh-shh-shh-ed" him right out the door.

He couldn't believe it. "Of all places, I thought sure this would be it," he muttered. "The Land of Lofty Vision – NOT! They oughta call it the Land of *Tunnel* Vision!"

This certainly was no place for him.

He was so depressed he didn't know what to do. He dragged himself back to the crossroads one last time and sat down under the signpost.

"There's no place left to go," he despaired. "I've gone to every land and they're all disasters.

"I can't go back to the Land of Business as Usual, and I won't go back to any of the others. It's hopeless, just hopeless."

Tired from his travels and discouraged from his experiences, A. Customer rested his head on his arms and closed his eyes.

"I might as well take a nap," he thought. "There's no place to go and nothing to do. I'll sleep for a while and decide what to do when I wake up."

And with that, he drifted off to sleep. His breathing slowed and his body relaxed as his sleep deepened. He felt like he was floating away on welcome clouds that wrapped him in soothing, fluffy softness. He sighed gently in the comfort of his slumber.

"Excuse me…are you all right?" A gentle voice interrupted his reverie.

"Huh….what?" A. Customer replied, groggy and confused as he first awoke.

"I saw you here, sleeping at the crossroads," the voice replied. "I thought perhaps you were lost. Can I help you?"

"I don't know if anyone can help me," A. Customer replied. "I've been everywhere and no one has helped."

"I understand how you must feel," the gentle voice responded.

A. Customer began to focus on her face now, a soft, gentle face that went with the soft, gentle voice. "I've been down all these roads myself, and they're all very disappointing."

"To say the least," A. Customer replied as he stood up, brushing the wrinkles from his clothes.

"Well, there's a road you didn't try, you know," she said. "That one, over there." And she pointed to an unmarked road.

It was big and wide and smooth, but there was no sign and no name.

"Huh? I never even noticed it," A. Customer asked. "Why is there no sign? Where does it lead?"

"It leads to the Land of Walk the Talk," she answered. "A very special place. They don't have a sign because they don't need one. They know that people like me will tell people like you."

"Will you show me the way?" A. Customer asked.

"Of course," she replied. "Come with me."

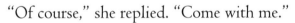

A. Customer noticed immediately that there were lots of other people traveling down the unmarked road.

"Seems to be a popular place," he remarked to his guide. "No wonder the road is so wide, with all these people going there."

"Yes," she replied. "When there's a place like the Land of Walk the Talk, word gets around."

As they drew closer, A. Customer heard the quiet, steady hum of people busy at work. He saw sparkling windows, attractive displays, and lots of people talking and smiling. Over the buzz of their conversations he heard the frequent "Ka-ching" of contented cash registers.

"This is amazing," he exclaimed, his eyes wide with wonder. "I've never seen anyplace like it! This is the Land of Walk the Talk?"

His guide nodded, smiling ever so slightly. She knew how unusual this place must look to A. Customer. It wasn't that long ago that she'd been in his place.

"Come, let me show you around." She gestured for him to follow her.

"Why do they call it the Land of Walk the Talk?" A. Customer asked. "That seems like an odd name."

"Well, that sign over there will help you understand," she said, pointing to a billboard across the way.

"There you can see the three principles that people live by here in the Land of Walk the Talk. Everyone knows them by heart, of course, but the sign helps people like you and me know what to expect, and how we'll be treated."

A. Customer looked at the sign and read it aloud to himself:

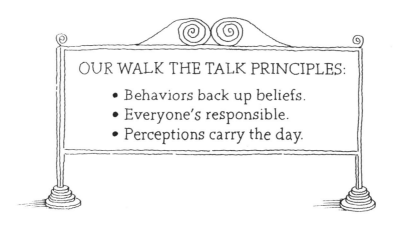

OUR WALK THE TALK PRINCIPLES:
- Behaviors back up beliefs.
- Everyone's responsible.
- Perceptions carry the day.

"Hmmm," he mused, turning back to his guide. "That sure sounds different from the Land of Business as Usual...and different from every other place I've been too! What exactly do they mean by these principles?"

"I understand your confusion," she said. "Let's see if we can find some examples here. For instance, see that man over there talking on the phone and making notes? Let's see if we can talk with him when he finishes his phone call."

As they approached his desk, they heard him saying goodbye. He stood up to greet them.

"Hi. I'm Ray F. Sunshine," he said. "How can I help you?"

A. Customer liked his warm, friendly smile.

"I'm new to this land," A. Customer said, "and I was wondering what you all mean by 'Behaviors back up beliefs.' Can you explain that for me?"

"Sure," Ray answered, "Have a seat. You see, the Land of Walk the Talk is built on a foundation of VALUES — a set of beliefs. Those three principles that you saw on the sign bring our values to life.

"Values and beliefs are words to live by. *But words to live by are just words, unless you truly live by them.*

"We don't just give lip service to our values — we actually live them every day in the way we do our jobs."

$\mathbb{A}$. Customer nodded, as Ray continued.

"For instance, here in the Land of Walk the Talk, one of our beliefs is that customers are our number one priority. One of the many behaviors that back up that belief is listening. And not just ordinary listening either, but listening from the heart — listening with genuine interest and a strong desire to help.

"It's the only way to find out what customers really want or need."

"I see," A. Customer replied. "And you just showed me, by the way you treated me, that your behavior backs up your belief. You're right, of course. It makes perfect sense. Words to live by are just words unless you live by them. Thank you, Ray, for explaining it so clearly."

"That was very interesting," A. Customer said to his guide. "Much better than the other lands I've seen. Now...what about the second principle, 'Everyone's responsible'?"

"Why don't we talk to that man over there," she answered. "The man in the pin-stripe suit, picking up that scrap of paper on the ground. Let's ask him what it means."

"Excuse me, sir," A. Customer said, as the man stood up, tossing the paper into a nearby trash can. "Could I ask you a question?"

"Of course," the man replied. "My name is C. E. O'Malley. How can I help you?"

"I'm new to your land," A. Customer said, "and I'm curious about what you mean when you say 'Everyone's responsible.' Can you explain it to me?"

"I'd be happy to," C. E. replied. "You see, we have kind of a funny saying here amongst ourselves: 'Nobody says it's somebody else's job.'

"What that means is that everyone here acts like an Owner. We know that Owners are pretty much responsible for everything. They handle whatever comes up, whenever it comes up."

"Does that mean that no one has job descriptions?" A. Customer asked. "Is there no division of labor?"

C. E. O'Malley shook his head. "We all have job descriptions," he said. "But we also know that it's often important to go above and beyond the job when the situation requires it."

"Wow," A. Customer marveled. "That's impressive. It must be empowering for the people who work here."

"Yes, indeed," C. E. O'Malley replied. "You can see it on people's faces and in everything they do. It's empowering and energizing to think and act like an Owner. We don't think of responsibility as a burden; we think of it as an honor. Responsibility gives everyone a sense of pride. It shows that what we do is truly important."

"Well, thank you very much for your time, sir," A. Customer said, as they shook hands. "I'll let you get back to work. I'm sure you're very busy."

"Never too busy to talk to A. Customer," O'Malley replied, smiling broadly. "Here's my card. If there's any-

thing else I can help you with, feel free to give me a call."

 He turned and headed back to his office as A. Customer glanced down at the card in his hand.

"Hey, look at this," he whispered loudly to his guide, "C. E. O'Malley is the President here... and he was picking up a piece of trash when we met him!"

His guide nodded as she smiled. "Yes, he really meant it when he said 'Everyone's responsible.'"

"Wow. I can hardly wait to learn about the third principle in the Land of Walk the Talk," A. Customer said eagerly. "'Perceptions carry the day.' Who should we talk to this time?"

"Let's ask her," the guide said as she pointed to a woman rushing through a doorway with a stack of order forms in her hand.

"She's hurrying to take care of those orders, but let's see if she'll talk to us."

A. Customer approached her cautiously and asked, "Excuse me, do you have a minute?"

"Certainly," the woman replied as she turned to shake A. Customer's hand. "I'm Tai Management. I'm in Operations. What can I do for you?"

"Well, I know you're busy. . ." A. Customer began.

"No problem," Tai said. "Just let me give these orders to our fulfillment team." Tai paused as she handed the forms to a woman standing behind a counter. "Now, how can I help you?"

"Well, I'm new here, and I wanted to know what you all mean by your principle, 'Perceptions carry the day.'"

"It's simple," Tai said. "Good service is in the eye of the served, not the server. Not only is it important what we actually *do* when you come here, it's important how you *think* we're doing. Nobody can read our minds, so they watch our behaviors. Then they interpret our behaviors and make judgements based on that."

"In short," Tai Management continued, "what I'm saying is that *we judge ourselves by our intentions, but we judge others by their behaviors.*

"How am I doing so far?"

"Could you give me an example?" A. Customer answered, a bit puzzled.

"OK," Tai said. "You see me rushing around here, very busy, getting stuff done. I think that I'm taking good care of my customers' orders — a positive perception on my part. But, if I fail to acknowledge you right away, when you first come in, then you might think that I'm too busy to help you, or worse yet, that I don't even care. Your perception would be negative. And whose perception is important?... *Yours* is.

"I always try to be aware of how my behavior is being seen by you. And I find out how you see it by asking you, 'How am I doing?' — like I did a minute ago."

A. Customer's eyes were wide open now, amazed and delighted with what he'd seen and heard.

"Thank you so much," he beamed at Tai Management. "I see exactly what you mean!"

"Let me know anytime I can help," Tai said. "Glad to be of service. And let me give you one of our catalogs. We've got great selection here, and great service!"

A. Customer turned to talk to his guide again.

"Well, I'm sold!" he announced happily.

"So now you understand why they call it the Land of Walk the Talk," she replied.

"In all those other lands their intentions are good and they say the right things, but their reality doesn't match their rhetoric. *They don't walk their talk.*

A. Customer nodded. "Yes, you're right. It's not that catchy slogans, promises of quality, and lofty vision aren't important – they are. But they're not enough."

"Exactly," his guide concurred. "People need to live what they profess to believe. If they don't walk their talk, they end up in the Land of Lip Service!"

A. Customer laughed at the image this brought to his mind. "I guess I shouldn't be laughing. This really is a serious matter. But it all seems so simple now. It makes me wonder why more lands haven't figured out how to walk their talk."

"I don't know," his companion mused, "I've often wondered the same thing myself."

"I can't thank you enough for bringing me here," A. Customer said. "There I was, sound asleep when you found me. And now I feel like I've awakened into a dream — A. Customer's dream come true!"

"My pleasure," she smiled. "As I said before, I've been through the same things as you."

There was a moment of silence as they looked at each other. A sense of mutual knowing slowly filled them both.

Finally, A. Customer broke the silence.

"You know," he started, "I just realized that I don't even know your name. You seem to know so much about me, but I didn't even ask your name. I apologize. I'm not usually so thoughtless. If it's not too late, would you tell me your name?

Her smile broadened into a grin.

"My name? My name is Customer-Too...

Ima Customer-Too, to be more precise."

THE END

Delivering Walk-the-Talk Service
In *Your* Organization

1. The road to the Land of Walk the Talk was unmarked — there was no sign. How did people find their way there? How do people find their way to *your* organization or business? How can you reduce your need to advertise by turning *your* customers into walking representatives of your company?

2. Everyone understands why providing excellent customer service is important to customers — and why it's important to organizations. But why is it good for employees? What's in it for *you*?

3. Walk the Talk is a familiar term, and it can mean different things to different people. What does Walking the Talk mean for the leaders and executives in your company? What does it mean for employees? What does it mean for *you*?

4. Why are catchy slogans, big promises, and lofty vision not enough to keep customers happy? Many companies think they're doing all the right things — yet their customers are not happy with the level of service they receive. What's missing?

5. The Land of Big Promises in our story was a land of technology. What are the "upsides" and the "downsides" of technology and its effect on customer service? Are there natural tradeoffs? How might you maximize

the advantages, while minimizing the disadvantages, with your organization's customers?

6. What are some of the obstacles that get in the way of everyone in your organization "walking their talk"? Can you make a list of those obstacles? Are there things on your list that *you* could do something about? Which obstacles are within your control to overcome or remove, and which obstacles are outside your influence?

7. Recall some of your own experiences as a customer. Have you ever had an experience where you felt like you were in the Land of Catchy Slogans? What was that like for you? What did you do about it? Have you ever felt like you were in the Land of Big Promises? What happened, and what did you do about it? Have you ever felt you were in the Land of Lofty Vision? What happened and what did you do about it?

8. Think about some wonderful experiences when you felt like you were doing business with the Land of Walk the Talk. What happened? How were you treated? What did the people there do that made you happy with their service?

9. What things can you learn from your own experiences as a customer to help you create the Land of Walk the Talk inside your company or organization?

Barbara "BJ" Gallagher Hateley is an accomplished management consultant and workshop leader — as well as a popular public speaker — specializing in customer service, change management, motivation, communication skills, creativity and innovation, workforce diversity, and specialized programs for women.

She is president of her own human resources training and consulting company, Peacock Productions, and has worked with scores of corporations, professional associations, nonprofit groups, and government agencies. Her clients include: DaimlerChrysler, Chevron, IBM, Volkswagen, Southern California Edison, Baxter Healthcare, and the American Lung Association.

A much-in-demand keynote speaker, BJ's presentations frequently highlight conferences and professional gatherings in the United States, Asia, Europe, and Latin America. In addition to publishing articles in *The L.A. Times*, *Training* magazine, and *Training & Development Journal*, she has authored numerous books. Her newest book is Witty Words from Wise Women: Quips, Quotes and Comebacks (Andrews McMeel, Kansas City, March 2001).

Also by BJ Gallagher Hateley:

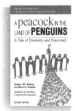

A Peacock in the Land of Penguins
This charming and engaging best-seller provides new insights on how to manage the increasing diversity of today's workforce and how to capture the talent, energy, and commitment of all employees.

Pigeonholed in the Land of Penguins
The first part of this powerful sequel is a memorable fable about stereotyping. The second part helps us focus on minimizing stereotyping in our lives and organizations. Together, the parts provide both inspiration and practical advice.

Order these popular resources or contact BJ Gallagher Hateley at
Peacock Productions
323.227.6205
www.peacockproductions.com
e-mail: PeacockHQ@aol.com

Eric Harvey is an internationally known speaker, author, and consultant in the areas of values-based business practices and organizational change.

With over 30 years of professional experience, he has authored eleven highly-acclaimed publications, including the best-selling Walk The Talk ... And Get The Results You Want. In addition, he has been recognized and published in scores of trade and professional journals including *Human Resource Executive, Industry Week, Wall Street Journal, Business Week, and Harvard Business Review.*

Eric is president of The WALK THE TALK Company — the Dallas-based human resources publishing, consulting, and training firm that works with values-based organizations internationally, including 84% of *Fortune* magazine's "World's Most Admired Companies."

Since 1977, Eric has shared his practical and compelling "Walk The Talk" message across the globe with corporations and professional groups ranging from General Electric, Caterpillar, and Pfizer to Qantas Airways, YMCA, and Cornell University.

<u>Also by Eric Harvey:</u>

180 Ways To Walk The Customer Service Talk
Packed with proven strategies and tips, this powerful handbook will benefit employees at every level — from front liners to call center reps, sales people, telemarketers, client services, and those "behind the scenes."

180 Ways To Walk The Recognition Talk
The time-tested techniques and practical strategies found in these pages will help you encourage positive, productive performance and build a "magnetic culture" that attracts and retains the best and brightest people.

Order these and other high-impact resources from
The WALK THE TALK® Company
1.888.822.9255
www.walkthetalk.com
e-mail Eric Harvey: info@walkthetalk.com

Customer at the Crossroads

Order Form

Call 1.888.822.9255

(See ORDERING INFORMATION in front of book for ordering options)

1-99	-	$9.95 each
100-499	-	$9.45 each
500-4,999	-	$8.95 each
5,000-9,999	-	$7.95 each
10,000 or more	-	$6.95 each

Copies _____

Book Total $ _____

*Shipping and Handling   +$ _____
(Continental U.S. - $4.00 plus 6% of "Book Total" above)

Subtotal $ _____

Texas Only - Sales Tax (8.25% of Subtotal)   +$ _____

TOTAL $ _____

*SHIPPING and HANDLING

Outside the continental U.S., please call 972.243.8863.
Orders shipped ground delivery to be received in 7-10 business days.
Next business day and second business day delivery are available.
Please call 1.888.822.9255 for information.

Name (MR/MRS/MS)_____

Title_____

Organization_____

Street Address_____
(do not use P.O. Box)

City_____State_____ Zip_____ Country_____

Phone (required to process order) (   ) _____ Ext. _____

Fax (   ) _____ e-mail _____

Purchase Order Number (if applicable) _____

☐ MasterCard   ☐ VISA   ☐ AMERICAN EXPRESS   ☐ Check or Money   ☐ Please Invoice
                                                Order Enclosed   (orders over $250 only)
                                                (Payable to: The WALK
                                                THE TALK Co,)

Account Number_____ Expiration Date_____
                                                        (month/year)
Signature_____

Prices effective January 2001 are subject to change without notice. Orders payable in U.S. dollars only.
Orders outside U.S. and Canada must be prepaid by credit card drawn on a U.S. bank. Orders under $250
must be prepaid by credit card, or money order. Restocking fee on returns within 30 days of original receipt.

THANK YOU FOR YOUR ORDER.